http://www.timreallylikes.com/creativitychecklist

Table Of Contents

My Free Gift To You

If you would like a free workbook, along with a 30 minute video and audio of me personally walking you through the 2kH Formula please visit: http://www.2khFormula.com/freegift

Once there, please provide a quality email address and I'll send you the workbook and walk-through video as my way of saying thanks for purchasing this book.

See you over at http://www.2khFormula.com/freegift

Tim

Houston, We Have A Problem ...

For years I've been known as the guy who outsources the majority of his content creation - including books published on Amazon.

In fact, the first time I sat down to write my first non-fiction book without an outsourcer was less than 30 days ago.

But I didn't plan on it being this way.

I was forced into creating my own content and in doing so stumbled upon the 2kH formula that changed my business forever...

When I set out to have my first nonfiction book outsourced, I followed all of the familiar steps.

I placed an ad on Elance, provided as much source material as possible, and looked for the best candidate within my budget.

I gave this guy everything he needed - an outline for the book, a 30 minute recording of me going over the content of the book, copies of my podcast (http://twodrinktim.com), and I even shared a short book formula I had paid thousands to learn.

Then I waited. And waited. And waited some more.

Finally, with 48 hours to spare until my deadline, I got the rough draft.

It was horrible. There was nothing but bland and boring writing along with critical pieces missing from the book.

I had two choices:

1. I could try and edit the book, get it back to the outsourcer, and pray everything drastically improved overnight.

or

2. I could write the book myself in less than 48 hours.

As I thought about my options, I couldn't help but laugh at the situation I had gotten myself into.

You see, I had promised a coaching class that I was going to show them the final draft during our final class together in just two short days.

These people had paid a lot of money to attend the class, and not coming through for them wasn't an option.

So I decided to get to work and write the book myself.

There was just one MAJOR problem - I had never written a book before, and the last time I had tried to write a ton of words in a short period of time was college, which was years ago.

Instead of panicking, I decided to develop a writing formula that would allow me to write my book in record time, with minimal effort and maximum results.

Speaking of results, allow me to share mine with you.

The first time I used this formula myself, I was able to do the following:

- Write at least 2,000 words per hour
- Write an entire book in 4 hours
- Have that same book published within 72 hours

That book, The Creativity Checklist (http://timreallylikes.com/creativitychecklist) went on to be an Amazon Best Seller and produced thousands of satisfied readers and a nice daily passive profit without me doing the heavy lifting.

I have no doubt this writing formula can do the same for you.

I urge you to pay attention, take notes and above all, put it into action. When you do, you'll immediately notice how you're producing more content in less time than ever before.

If you're a writer (blog, book, article, etc.) this 2kH formula will help you.

If you hire others to create content for you, feel free to share this information with them and watch as their productivity soars and production increases for you.

There is truly something for everyone with the 2kH formula.

Sound good? Well, let's get to work.

There is that dreaded 'W' word. Sorry to disappoint any wannabe push button millionaires but this formula won't work if you don't. It may take a few minutes to get used to using the formula, but I promise that once you do, you'll see how big of a benefit it produces in every area of your writing, and never look back.

Let's begin.

Why You Should Use The 2kH Formula

Have you ever struggled to share your thoughts or put words on paper?

Have you ever stared at a blank screen, then looked at your clock while remembering your impending deadline, and wondered how in the world you were going to accomplish it all?

Do you struggle to find the time to write and always seem to miss out on the "perfect" writing location when trying to do so?

If so, welcome, you've come to the right place and I know those feelings all too well.

That's what first attracted me to outsourcing my work because I got so burnt out worrying about those same things.

But sometimes, depending on others can bite you in the ass.

That's what happened to me and it happened at the worst possible time.

Imagine having a room full of your highest paying clients anxiously waiting on you to deliver the final book you promised them.

Then imagine watching your entire game plan to deliver that book crumble before your eyes and having to start from square one with less than 48 hours til your deadline.

I don't have to imagine it, because that's exactly what happened to me.

I had hired an outsourcer to create my first nonfiction book, The Creativity Checklist (http://timreallylikes.com/creativitychecklist) I gave him everything I thought he needed.

I gave him ...

A 30 minute video of me walking him through the Creativity Checklist. I did this so he could simply listen to the video and my explanation of everything and then write the book.

Access to all of my Two Drink Tim Podcast (http://twodrinktim.com). I did this so he could listen to them and capture my voice, because I write just like I talk and I try to keep everything conversational - just like you and I are having a beer together and I'm explaining something really cool to you.

A nonfiction writing formula that I had paid thousands to learn. I wanted him to use a simple-to-understand formula to lay out the book in perfect order.

Despite all this (and more), the outsourcer failed miserably.

The rough draft was barely readable, lacked more than half the information I wanted in it, and sounded nothing like I wanted it to.

Because I was so close to my deadline I had little choice but to get to work and write the book myself.

I'll admit, I was scared.

This was my first nonfiction book, I hadn't written anything of great length in years, and I had never produced a book within this time frame.

I clearly had my work cut out for me. Because I was so short on time, I couldn't spend much of it pondering, so instead I decided to take massive action and in the process created the 2kH writing formula.

It's the same formula I used to create this book as well and I'm proud to report it has a 100% success rate for me and the people I've shared it with prior to today.

So let's talk about the 2kH formula and see exactly what it is and how you can use it in your own life and business.

What is the 2kH Formula?

The 2kH writing formula is a system that I came up with that allows you to write at least 2,000 words per hour.

When you use it, you'll notice your production and productivity increase massively while working less and less.

In fact, the first book I used this system on was created in less than 4 hours. It went on to be an Amazon best seller and has produced a steady passive income for me to this day.

The best part about this system is that it can be learned quickly, and once learned you can begin using it at once. It doesn't rely on a ton of fancy software or programs and it can be used for any type of writing you can throw at it.

I've used it primarily for nonfiction writing, but I know writers who produce fiction, screenplays, articles, blog post, and more that could benefit from this formula.

At its core, the 2kH writing formula boils down to these five major areas:

1. Coming up with ideas
2. Outlining your project
3. The secret method
4. Your writing environment
5. Doing the work

Let's look at each of these major areas individually.

Part 1: Coming Up with Ideas

Whenever I tell people I'm a writer one of the first things the majority of people respond with is this:

"That's awesome, I wish I could write a book, but I don't know anything important like you do."

How wrong they are.

If you've ever felt that way (and who hasn't felt that way at least once in their life) I'm going to help you smash that limiting belief right now.

Here's how.

Take out a piece of paper and fold it into 4 equal squares.

Then I want you to write the following headers (1 per square):

1. Previous & Current Job
2. Known skills
3. Life accomplishments
4. People you know

Next I want you to get away from the computer and all distractions and spend 5 minutes on each square writing down anything that comes to mind.

Don't think, don't edit, just do it.

In less than 20 minutes I bet you'll have at least a page overflowing with ideas.

By the way, I practice what I preach so allow me to share a few of my results with you so we can move on to the next step.

Previous & Current Job
- Wedding Photographer
- Bookkeeper
- Small business manager
- Clinical / Stage Hypnotist
- Insurance adjuster
- Internet marketing
- Author

Known skills
- Photography
- Bookkeeping
- Managing others
- Hypnosis
- Insurance adjusting
- How to market products, build an email list, make products,
- How to write and market books

Life accomplishments
- Lost 50 pounds
- Debt free in my 30s
- Paid my house off in my 30s
- Wrote a bestselling book
- Built a business from scratch that has sold over 1 million dollars worth of products

I won't even bother with listing the people I know because this exercise is for your benefit.

Once you have your list completed, I want you to ask yourself this life changing question:

"Which one of these would someone else be willing to pay me $3 to learn?"

Read that question again and then lets talk about it.

One of the biggest mistakes I see new authors make is thinking that they have to have life-changing and amazing results before anyone will listen to them.

Wrong. Wrong. Wrong.

Here's the sad truth - the mediocre majority do very little with their lives.

Here's why that's great news for you - the mere act of doing something over nothing makes you stand out from them, and makes people naturally want to follow you.

Here's the other thing to consider - people are more likely to believe a small result instead of a big one.

Think about it for a second - if someone told you they know how they could make an extra $100 a month would you believe them? Most likely.

Now what if that same person said they could show you how to make an extra $100,000 a month. Now would you believe them? Probably not.

You are not alone. People are more skeptical than ever and as a result, people are looking for small wins in their lives over major makeovers.

All of this plays into your hands perfectly.

With all this in mind, go back to your worksheet and start circling things that you think someone would pay you $3 to learn.

Know an exercise that helps people with back pain? Circle it.

Know how to cook healthy meals for your family, for cheap? Circle it.

Have you lost weight, paid off debt, started a cool side project, created an amazing relationship with your kids and/or spouse? Circle all of them.

If you need a little more guidance, keep this in mind.

A majority of the money spent on books, programs, courses, etc. (like 80% of the money) is spent on improving health, wealth, relationships, and business and hobbies.

If you have a circle around one of those topics you're well on your way to success.

Now, for the negative nellies out there, let's talk about if the opposite happens.

Let's say after going through your entire list you have nothing circled and don't think you have anything to write about.

Now I seriously doubt that you've done nothing with your life, but we'll play it your way for now.

So if you truly have nothing circled and nothing to write about I have GREAT news for you.

Your life is about to become amazing.

Why?

Because you're going to do something you've always wanted and get paid to do so.

How? Well, I'm glad you asked...

If you feel like you have nothing to share with the world, I want you to take an additional few minutes and write down a list of things you want to accomplish.

Maybe you want to lose weight, meditate, have a better sex life (hopefully with someone other than yourself), create a business, write a book, etc.

Once you've created that list I want you to go back and find the ONE THING that excites you the most.

After you've done that, it's time to get to work.

For the next 30 days I want you to focus on that one thing.

First, I want you to buy a few books and programs about the subject. Listen to a few podcasts or watch some video interviews with experts on YouTube.

Then I want you to actually study them, take notes and develop a game plan to start doing it.

Next I want you to do the most important step - actually do the damn thing you want to.

Finally, I want you to record everything you do somewhere. It can be a blog, a simple word document, Post-It-Notes, smoke signals, etc. Write down the books you read, the courses you listened to, the programs you tried, the successes, the frustrations, the failures, and the victories.

I don't care how you record it, as long as you do it.

I promise you at the end of 30 days the transformation will be amazing.

Then guess what's next ....

It's time to tell the world about it.

Think about it - just 30 days ago you were a complete newbie and now you've accomplished something, or are well on your way to doing so.

Who would want to know about that, you ask?

Everyone.

Every day there are thousands of people searching for information on how to get started with the same subject you just spent the last 30 days practicing.

Who do you think they'd like to learn from - someone who was just in their shoes or someone whose results seem unachieveable to them?

By the way, if this all seems like too much work, allow me to share a simple shortcut with you - the success of others.

Remember the fourth square I asked you to fill out - people you know.

Well, there's a reason for that. You see, even if you feel like you know nothing chances are, you know someone who has done something remarkable.

As I think about my immediate circle of friends and family I have ...

- A family member who lost 100+ pounds
- Several friends with successful offline businesses
- A family member who started a successful business in their 60s
- I know someone who has totally changed their life in almost every major area

Remember how you were all modest about your accomplishments and didn't think anyone cared enough to notice?

Chances are these people feel the same way. If they do, now is your chance to help them (and profit in the process).
Here's what you could do.

You could approach them and tell them how impressed you are about whatever topic you want to write about. Then come up with a list of questions you'd like to ask them and do so. Record the conversation (with their permission, of course) and now you have something to write about.

The best part about this strategy is that you don't have to do anything (except write about it) to share the results they achieved.

Now that you've got those ideas circled and picked the one you want to write about, let's move on to Part 2.

Part 2: Outlining Your Idea

For years I only wrote when I felt like it. And when I did write it was off the cuff and with very little preparation or outline.

While I was successful, I ran into a lot of challenges as well.

When I didn't feel like it - I didn't write. Because of that, there were long delays between projects because I didn't feel inspired. So I drifted and drifted some more, waiting and waiting for inspiration to hit me.

When inspiration finally did hit, I'd sit and stare at a blank computer screen - not sure where to begin, not sure what to include, and not sure where to go to properly express my ideas.

My work suffered and my stress level was constantly rising because of it.

Because I had such a tight deadline for this project I didn't have the luxury of waiting for inspiration to hit or writing when I felt like it.

I had to create a system that allowed me to pull ideas into a proven formula and achieve the desired result. I needed something easy to understand, quick to implement, with a proven track record of success.

The first thing I did was use the Creativity Checklist
(http://timreallylikes.com/creativitychecklist).

It's impossible to go over all 8000+ words in the book, but I will briefly paraphrase it here.

I created the Creativity Checklist after years of struggling to properly express my ideas to others.

It's an 11 step system I now use with every idea I have. The first time I used it, it made me over ten thousand dollars.

It allows me to effortlessly share my ideas with my staff, customers, outsourcers, and more.

It gives me instant clarity and makes the following steps even easier.

Here are the questions I ask:

1. What problem does your product/service solve?
2. What proof do you have that it works?
3. What will be included with your product/service?
4. What is your story behind the product/service?
5. How recent or believable is your product or service?
6. What are the features/benefits of using your product or service?
7. Who are your competitors for this product or service?
8. What other income possibilities - recurring or one time only - are there in addition to this product or service?
9. What are the hooks/angles we can take with this product/service?
10. What testimonials or third party data do you have about your product or service?
11. How much time and/or money did it take you to develop your product or service?

For a more detailed explanation, a complete breakdown of the system and a 30 minute video walk-through along with seeing the checklist in action visit:
http://www.timreallylikes.com/creativitychecklist

You can also find the book on Amazon by searching "the Creativity Checklist".

Once I finish the Creativity Checklist, I use a very simple, nonfiction writing formula to help complete my outline.

The Nonfiction Writing Formula

This was the first writing formula I learned years ago and it's been responsible for over a million dollars worth of products and services being sold.

I also used the same formula to help create my nonfiction bestselling book.

The nonfiction writing formula is: Why / What / How / If - Then

Lets talk about each step of it.

Step 1: Why

This is the first part of any nonfiction report or book I produce. In it, I simply explain why the reader should listen to me and why they should use whatever I'm sharing with them.

For instance, with this book I explained my situation and the nightmare of hiring an outsourcer. I then shared my results using the 2kH formula. This was intentional. I wanted you not only to understand how the 2kH formula came to be, but that it has been "battle tested" and proven prior to sharing it with others.

By doing that I put the reader (and you) at ease and also helps establish my credibility to share the information with them. I'm not some guy who's regurgitating something he heard about, I'm sharing something that I've personally used successfully.

Remember a few pages back where I talked about the fact that merely doing something makes you stand out from those doing nothing. The same applies here. It also helps establish trust with your readers because you've already done the hard work for them and are now sharing your winning formula/system/diet with them.

Step 2: What

In the second part you lay out whatever you're writing about completely. I like to do this using a step-by-step breakdown of the major topic.

If your topic lends itself to steps, then it's pretty simple to do. If it's a different type of topic, then you'll want to use my 5x5 formula to explain everything.

Here's what the 5x5 formula is ...

You simply take a major topic (in this example weight loss) and break it down into the 5 major parts or steps people would need to achieve the desired result.

So for weight loss lets say these are the 5 major steps:

- Diet
- Exercise
- Sleep
- Accountability
- Staying on course / Getting back on track

Once you have those 5 major categories, you then break each one of them down further.

Let's take sleep from the previous example.

Sleep is the major category, but I would create 3 to 5 minor subcategories under it.

It would look like this:

Sleep
- Why sleep is so important
- Figuring out how much sleep you need
- What to do before you sleep
- Your sleeping environment
- How to keep track

If you want, you can take it a step further and do sub subcategories, but honestly I rarely go that far.

When you're done your outline should look like this:

Major Topic: Weight loss

Part 1: Diet
- Subcategory #1
- Subcategory #2
- Subcategory #3
- Subcategory #4
- Subcategory #5

I usually do this part on paper, but if you'd rather use technology to your advantage find a mind mapping program like Xmind, Freemind, or iThoughts to use.

The great thing about creating an outline prior to doing any actual writing is it gives you time to organize your thoughts, ensure you're covering everything you want, and create a "flow" to the book, article, or blog post.

Once you have the outline of the What section, it's time to focus on the most important part of the outline.

Step 3 - How

To me, this is the most important part of the outline because it talks about how to implement the idea you're trying to convey to others.

Notice during this book how I've given several suggestions on how to create a list of ideas, how to outline your book, and more.

It's all done deliberately. How many times have you read a great idea and thought - "I'd love to do that, but how do I get started?"

That's why the how section is so powerful. Up until this point you've shared with your readers why they should listen to you, and the complete system or idea, but in this section you're going to go from idea to implementation.

Make it as simple as possible for people to get started. List anything and everything you think will help them. Software, books, programs, systems and more.

Pay special attention later in this book to the section on "How To Use The 2kH Formula" and use that as a model to create your own successful how section.

Did you see what I did just there?

I just shared with you an example of how you can get started - by modeling my process.

Something to remember is that people hate to look stupid and make mistakes. The more you can explain not only what they should do, but how they can accomplish each step, the more they believe in their own ability to do so.

The more they believe in their own ability, the better the chance they will actually use whatever you're sharing and get the desired result. The more people who get amazing results, the more people they tell, and so on.

It really can be a snowball effect if you position your how section correctly.

Step 4 - If / Then

This part of your outline is going to cover both the good and bad of whatever you're writing about.

For instance, if there are certain hiccups that people normally encounter with weight loss here is the perfect place to address them and tell the reader how to overcome it.

Let's say I have a book on low carb weight loss.
One of the things I might address is how to overcome sugar cravings and healthy or safe alternatives to traditional snacks.

Another example that would fit perfectly here is to talk about when someone struggles or fails.

Keeping with the low carb weight loss example, you might want to include what people should do if they have a cheat meal or fall off the diet bandwagon.

You won't be able to cover them all, but if you can address the top 3 to 5 challenges most people encounter you'll be doing your reader a great service.

By including as many of these suggestions as possible you're able to let the reader know how to move past difficult challenges and if they want to get even better results, how to scale them up successfully.

Best of all, using this 4 part outlining formula you'll neatly organize your major and minor concepts for you to begin the next part - the secret sauce.

Once you feel like you have your outline done, I highly recommend you using a mindmapping program like Xmind to organize everything. It will also make this next step even easier.

Part 3: The Secret Sauce

I can honestly say I've never heard anyone talk about or share what I'm about to with you. I'm not saying that they haven't, I've just never heard it before.

I also think this was the one thing I did that had the biggest impact on my ability to write 2,000 words an hour and create a best selling book in four hours.

Here it is.

Once I'm done doing an outline I take the raw information and input it into a Mindmap.

I typically use Xmind (which is a free mind mapping software) and create a simple-to-follow map that lays out the major parts of the book I want to write.

You can grab the Mindmap I created for this book here: http://www.2khformula.com/freegift

After I have the Mindmap laid out and I'm happy with the "flow" of the outline, I use a screen recording program like Camtasia or Screencast-O-Matic.

Next I plug in my headset - a Logitech G930 and get to work.

I use the screen recording software to capture my voice and record the Mindmap at the same time.

Finally, I "write" my book by walking through each section of the Mindmap.

I usually start with an introduction (which usually a story) and share how I came to create and use whatever I'm talking about.

Think back to the start of this book - how did it begin?

By me telling you about my nightmare involving outsourcing and problem I quickly found myself in.

I did so intentionally.

You see, it's been proven over the course of history that people learn best through stories, so I do my best to use them whenever possible. It makes things easier to understand and doesn't come off as bland and sterile textbook writing in the process.

Here's something else I try to do in the introduction – show future success.

Go back to the beginning of the book again, notice how I started with a story and then went on to share my success with the 2kH writing formula.

Things like ....
- The ability to write 2,000 words per hour
- The fact I wrote a book in 4 hours
- That book became an Amazon Best Seller

Again, I did this deliberately. People are more willing to give something a shot if someone else has taken the risk first and achieved a desireable result.

Think about that - we ask for recommendations from others all the time. But what are we really looking for when we ask? Someone to say, "Don't worry, I've used them / done that, and had success with it."

In short, we're looking for a fall guy or a scapegoat, just in case something goes wrong.

"Well, Tim said he had used this system before with great success "

Another benefit of sharing your success in the beginning is that it positions you as an expert in the subject.

My story:
- I shared my story of woe and struggle
- I shared my plan to get out of it
- I shared my success as a result

How could anyone say that I wasn't an expert, qualified to teach a subject that I had experienced all three phases of and been successful in overcoming?

By including stories of success, the reader can't help but put themselves in your place during the story and start imagining their own success.

Admit it, before you started reading this book you might not have thought about writing a book, starting a blog, creating an information product, or any of the other 100 ideas now racing through your head ... but now, you've got a head full of ideas that the 2kH system can help you with.

Once I'm done with the introduction, I typically start off talking about why you should use the product, system, or service I'm going to talk about at length. I usually get super creative and create a section entitled "Why You Should Use XXX"

A lot of the "why you should use" section covers the same main points as the introduction, but it gives more supporting statements and facts about why you should use X and the benefits of doing so.

After the Why section, I break down the entire program/system/service in the What section. The purpose of the What section is to lay out everything in a step-by-step sequence. In the creativity checklist I simply listed all 11 questions in the system and gave a deeper explanation of each question.

Next I move on to the How section which explains how to implement the product/system/service I just laid out in the what section. Again, I get super creative and use chapter titles like "How To Use ..."

In the How section I try to explain exactly how I used the system/product/service the first time and how I am using it currently. My goal is to give enough of an explanation so that the reader can achieve success by simply following what I did. Even if they aren't successful doing exactly what I do, they still have a starting place or ground zero to get started with the How section.

Once I'm finished with the How section, I wrap things up in the If/Then section. In this section I try to give tips and suggestions for when things go right and when things go wrong. Here is where I'll share a few hurdles I might have encountered and how I overcame them. I'll also share how I plan to scale things up if the product/service/system proves successful.

Above all, I want to leave the reader with a sense of "hey, I can do this" more than "Tim Castleman is amazing." By sharing my struggles and successes, I try to bond with the reader and show them how I was able to overcome the odds with whatever I'm writing about.

If you really want to cement this process, I recommend adding a fast action section or a quick start guide at the end of your book. In that section, you would simply recap the major points of the book and suggest the first few steps for the reader to take once they're done with your book.

So, here's a quick recap of our nonfiction writing formula and the resulting mindmap:

Introduction
- This section established who you are, your story of struggle and eventual success

Why
- This section explains why people should listen to you and why they should use the product/service/system you're going to be writing about

What
- This section explains the product/service/system in its entirety and breaks it down into individual parts or steps for the reader to get a better understanding.

How
- This section shares how you put the product/service/system into action and the results you achieved with it. I like to break down my action steps into simple milestones showing exactly what I do. The goal here is to give the reader everything they need to do to go from thinking about using it, to actually doing so.

Remember, people are scared and looking for someone else to take the first step for them. The more you can break things down, the more willing they are to follow in your footsteps.

If/Then
- This section shares what to do if things go right or wrong. Talk about common hurdles and how you overcame them. Show how you are planning to scale things up now that you have things figured out. If you really want to impress them, share with them a fast action guide explaining exactly how they can get started.

Regardless of what you talk about, keep it simple to understand and explain to others. I just checked and according to my editing, and this book is currently being written at an eighth grade reading level.

The reason I want it like that is I'm not trying to impress anyone with 10 cent words or above-their-head thinking. In fact, as people read my work, my goal is to have them imagine us just having a simple conversation where I'm sharing my knowledge with them over a beer.

Keep the fancy words in worthless college textbooks and boring law reviews - when you're writing for others keep things as simple and easy-to-understand as possible.

The real benefit of talking through your book is creating the conversational tone of your writing. It also ensures that your stories, ideas, checklists, etc. flow naturally from one bullet point to the next.

For instance, while recording the Mindmap for this book, I came across a section that seemed out of place so late in the book so I switched it to a location that made more sense towards the beginning.

Switching that section in the outline prior to writing allowed me to stay in flow when it came time to write and decreased my need to stop and think while writing.

Once I'm happy with the outline and the various sections contained in it, I hit the record button and ramble on as long as necessary over the major topics in the book.

While I'm not "writing" the book per say, I am cementing the various parts of it in my brain. As an added benefit, I'm also creating a video that has a high perceived value to the end reader. I usually offer the video, along with the Mindmap, as an ethical bribe at the beginning of the book.

You might have noticed this at the beginning of this book:

My Free Gift To You

If you would like a free workbook, along with a 30 minute video and audio of me personally walking you through the 2kH Formula please visit: http://www.2khFormula.com/freegift

Once there, please provide a quality email address and I'll send you the workbook and walk-through video as my way of saying thanks and purchasing this book.

See you over at http://www.2khFormula.com/freegift

Tim

When you enter your email address you're sent the same video I used as my video outline for this book. In it you can hear me walking through each step and chapter prior to doing any actual writing of the book.

I've even been known to sell that same video and Mindmap on its own to cement it's value. For instance, I sell the Creativity Checklist as a stand-alone system at creativitychecklist.com

By doing so, it puts a real world value on the free gift and gives me another possible income stream for the book.

Let me share one more thing with you. By the time I get done recording the video I've almost worked myself into a frenzy. I've spent time doing a Creativity Checklist, I've outlined the book, and created a rough draft on video with the Mindmap.

The entire process in the last paragraph is what allows me to create content and write rapidly about it. For instance, I wrote the first part of this book last week (4,000 words in 2 hours) and have just now sat back down in front of the computer.

Even though a week has passed, because I did so much pre-work, I was able to sit down at the computer and knock out another 2,000 words in an hour. If I get stuck or stumble, all I have to do is simply refer to the Mindmap or watch the video again to keep going.

That is, once I take care of the next step - creating the perfect writing environment.

Part 4 - Creating The Perfect Writing Environment

I don't think there is a one-size-fits-all approach to creating the perfect writing environment. The goal is for YOU to create the perfect environment for YOU to succeed in.

For years I tried other people's suggestions and tips on how and where to write and now I've finally got a system in place that works for me.

If you're just getting started, I suggest you try my approach first and then adjust as necessary for your needs. Don't think for one second you're going to offend me (or anyone else) by creating something totally unique, as long as it works for you.

Here's what works for me.

I have two places I primarily write these days:

- At home
- At the coffee shop

At home I'm blessed with my own home office - which I know is a luxury for most. I have a triple monitor setup connected to my desktop computer, which is all housed on a butcher block desk I bought from Amazon.

On one screen I have my outline and on another I have the video rough draft, ready to play at a moment's notice. But I keep those screens off unless I need them and instead focus all my attention on the main screen, which shows me the Google Document I'm writing my book in.

There are a ton of writing software and programs out there, but I try to keep things deliberately simple by using Google Drive as my writing software. The best part is I can write at home and when I get bored or need a change of scenery I simply save my writing to the cloud and pick it up on my laptop within seconds.

When writing at home, I try to eliminate as many distractions as possible. I close down any instant messaging software (like Skype), logout of Facebook, Twitter, Gmail, and if necessary actually use programs like StayFocused to block the internet while writing.

Next I take my cell phone and switch it into airplane mode so I'm not disturbed by text messages, phone calls, or any other potential distractions. If I don't plan on listening to music, I even go as far as to put my phone in another room.

Out of sight, out of mind and less chance to get distracted by social media or video games.

During the day, things are pretty quiet where I live, but that doesn't stop me from using noise canceling headphones when I write.

If you like over-the-ear headphones, I would suggest Bose QC15 headphones or Audio Technica ATH 40.

If you like in-ear headphones, grab yourself a pair of Shure se215.

The goal here is to keep focused on actually writing and not get distracted by a ringing telephone, knock on the door, or neighbor's dog barking.

As far as my desk surface I like to keep things clean and simple. No food, just some handwritten notes, a drink, and headphones. Everything else is unnecessary.

If you're not able to have a similar or quiet working environment at home, a coffee shop might be the next best thing.

I typically work out of coffee shops a few times per week. I find there is a science to working in a noisy environment while still being productive.

Here's what works for me.

I like to take a Chromebook with me to the coffee shops. If you're not familiar, a Chromebook is simple laptop that only runs Chrome OS. It is severely limited to only Chrome services, extensions, and functions and that's exactly how I want it.

By taking the Chromebook I can't load any software, games, or chat services on it. I can only surf the net and write. With my Chromebook I keep just two tabs open - one for music and one for writing.

I take my Shure se215 noise cancelling headphones and block out the world with a specific music playlist I enjoy while writing.

The playlist (entitled writing) is a collection of 10 to 12 songs I enjoy listening to. The catch is this - I usually only listen to this playlist while writing and since the songs are on repeat, I hear them again and again and again.

The playlist acts as a trigger after using it for so long. My body knows its time to write when it hears the first beat of the first song. Because my brain is familiar with the songs after a few tracks the words become irrelevant and instead help block out the noise around me.

As an experiment, today I tried to listen to some random music while writing. I found myself paying attention to the songs and my brain struggling to understand them while trying to write at the same time. When I switched over to the playlist, the writer's block disappeared and the words started to flow freely again.

When I'm at the coffee shop I order a drink (they'll eventually get to know you and have it ready when you walk in the door), use the facilities and set up my work station. Once the headphones go in and the music starts, the world disappears.

I try to get in a solid hour or two writing session no matter where I write at. I find it takes a few minutes to get up to full speed writing and by eliminating the distractions and giving yourself long periods of time you can really crank out a lot of content quickly.

For instance, the first writing session for this book was only two hours long but produced 4500 words. The second writing session will only be for 90 minutes or so, but already I've added an additional 3000 words to the book.

That's the power of having the perfect writing environment.

One more thing I want to talk about when it comes to writing is you. Specifically, how you feel when you get ready to write. Are you sick, tired, distracted?

If so, your results may be different because you're not in your optimal state.

While it would be nice to tell you to take a nap, drink some coffee, or focus more, I know that's not always possible. What I will say is do your best to take care of yourself. I'd much rather take a nap and then write for a shorter period of time than to write while I'm exhausted.

I'd also cut yourself some slack when you're sick or life events keep you away from the computer. As an old friend use to say – there is no point in trying to push rope. Instead of getting upset or frustrated, I just use these moments to build my desire for the next time I'm able to write.

One thing I've been toying with is having a certain day (or time of day) that I block off for doing nothing but writing. Everyone around me knows what that time is and unless something critical happens, they leave me alone.

No one is going to make your writing a priority, unless you do first.

Speaking of writing, lets talk about the actual process of getting you writing at least 2,000 words per hour.

Part 5 - How To Write At Least 2,000 Words Per Hour

You have all the tools, tips, and techniques I use to get ready to write.

You know how to outline, why you should record your rough draft, and how to set up the perfect writing environment. Now lets talk about doing the work.

The first thing I do to encourage 2,000 words per hour is make it a game. Meaning I sit down at the computer and instead of stressing out or worrying about how many words I can produce I simply ask myself, "I wonder how many words I can write in the next 60 minutes?"

Then I make note of the time and start writing. By making it a game, I keep things fun and slightly competitive without beating myself up. For instance, in the last hour I wrote 2,234 words and I'm on pace to match that, if not beat it this hour.

To keep myself focused and motivated I take a screenshot of my word count at the beginning of my writing time and at the hour mark.

If you're using Google Docs you can get your word count by simply pressing Shift-Ctrl-C at the same time.

Once I know where I'm starting, every 15 minutes or so I'll check my word count. Doing so allows me to know how close I am to my 2000 words in an hour (I'm 928 words in 29 minutes so far this hour). By knowing that I'm a little under the 2k pace this hour, subconsciously I speed up and focus more to meet the goal.

In addition to making it a game, and keeping track of my productivity, I also like to reward myself often. When I'm at a coffee shop that usually means I get a refill or a new drink once I've hit the

2k mark and when I'm at home, I usually allow a few minutes of mindless social media surfing once I put in my time at hitting my goal.

By rewarding the behavior, I am conditioning myself to do more of it. Yes, I'm turning myself into Pavlov's dog one hour at a time. If you need some additional motivation and don't find positive reinforcement helpful, consider adding consequences into the mix.

Here's what I mean. Years ago when I wanted my staff to increase productivity, I came up with a simple plan - accomplish everything on your to-do list today, and get $10. But, when they didn't accomplish everything on their list, we took that $10 and donated it to social cause they hated.

For instance, when I didn't get my work done, I had to donate to the Westboro Baptist Church - an organization I can't stand to see in existence. As funny as it might sound, sometimes the pain of having to do something like that can be more motivating than the reward of accomplishing something.

I can't tell you how many times people stayed late or worked on the weekends to finish projects simply to avoid having to donate to a cause they hated. That's the power of negative consequences. The key here is to not overdo it.

In the past when I've had a major goal I wanted to accomplish I've tried to have major negative consequences associated with it. Stuff like a funny dance video posted on Facebook, the loss of a technology gadget for a month, large financial donations to groups I hate, etc. What I found was the thought of having to go through with those punishments were enough to keep me from even attempting the goal.

Moderation is key and it's better to die by a thousand papercuts than one major one.

Here's another huge tip for increasing your word count - write first, edit second.

When I'm writing the only thing I usually stop for is to correct a misspelled word or gather my thoughts to move forward. I do all of my editing after the fact. Neil Strauss shared this philosophy with me a few years ago:

The first draft is for the writer.
The second draft is for the editor.
The third draft is for the reader.

Focus on producing the best work possible first, then edit it afterwards. If you just can't bring yourself to write without editing, consider some distraction-free software that only allows you to write and not edit at the same time.

If that doesn't work, do what my friend Colin does - write drunk and edit sober. The key is to quiet that little voice in your head while the good creative energy is flowing. I also find that because you write so fast for a few a hours you use all your energy just keeping up, you don't have any to spare for editing.

If all else fails, hire an external editor and let them worry about the nouns, pronouns, spelling and punctuation. After all, you're the writer and your job is to create content, not destroy it before showing it to anyone else.

What I like to do when I think I'm finished with a project is print it out and review it.

I take the time to read it out loud to see where readers might get hung up on certain words, paragraphs, or ideas.

Then I usually ask a close friend or my assistant to edit my writing. Be careful when doing this that you don't get someone who would be afraid of telling you the truth. Friends and family might be afraid of hurting your feelings by being honest with you.

To overcome that I tell them that I want them to be brutally honest with me and actually encourage them to point out everything they see. Then it's up to me to take that feedback and make the necessary changes.

Finally, I hire an editor (you can find them on Fiverr or Elance) to give a final spit and polish.

The great thing is by the time all of the editing is done, I'm usually a few days removed from my writing and can look at it with fresh eyes again.

I make a final round of revisions and edits and then consider it good enough.

Notice I didn't say perfect. Perfection is the enemy of progress. When things are 90% "perfect" I put my writing out into the world (blog post, ebook, etc.).

Once I do that, readers let me know if I missed something, need to expand on something, or any other errors I might have made. In this day and age NOTHING is permanent and with a few clicks of the mouse almost anything can be changed.

Not to mention when you address the issues your readers bring up to you, you only stand to build even more trust and respect with them.

Now that you know all the parts of the formula, let's talk about the best way for you to get started.

Getting Started

Now that you know everything about the 2kH formula, let's talk about the most important part - getting started using it.

Knowledge without action and achievement is just a wasted opportunity and I don't want that for you.

So here's my suggestion for using and getting the most out of the 2kH formula.

Step 1: Create a list of ideas you want to write about
Step 2: Create an outline for the content you want to share
Step 3: Create a Mindmap and video walking yourself through the content
Step 4: Block off 60 minutes to write and create a writing environment that will help you stay focused.
Step 5: Keep track of when you start and do a word count check every 15 minutes to keep yourself accountable
Step 6: Reward yourself every time you take action. This will only help reinforce the habit and keep you motivated to do it again.

I know that list looks simple on paper, but it can be anything but in real life.

When I first talked with my wife about becoming self employed she was less than thrilled with the idea. It was only after we talked about the sacrifices we'd both be willing to make in order for it to happen that she understood why I wanted to work for myself and finally supported me.

Sometimes it meant she went to bed hours before I did. Occasionally it meant I got up before everyone else to get my time in. Once in a while it caused an argument between us.

But no matter what she supported me, because she knew how important it was to me.

If you find yourself running into the same situation, I suggest you sit down with your loved ones and explain what you're trying to accomplish and why you're trying to do it.

Share the big picture or goal you have. Show them that it's not just hours of mindless tapping away at the keyboard, but that you have something bigger in mind.

Once they buy into your idea, it's up to you to be militant about getting to work and accomplishing your goal.

Don't worry what others might say or think along the way - they don't understand you like I do. That's why they live the life they do.

I remember years ago my friends laughed at my Geo Metro I drove in college and then the Chevy Cavalier I "upgraded" to when I got my first real job.

They didn't understand why I skipped out on the fancy vacations, high end vehicles, and drinking on the weekends.

I spent a few years living like no one else, so later I could live like no one else (thank you Dave Ramsey for those powerful words).

The only thing that has changed for them is time.

But not for me. You see, I saved my money, I was able to quit my job, and in the process I built a new business from nothing to 6 figures in less than 24 months.

I was able to pay off all of my debt and pay off my house by age 31.

None of that would have been possible if I'd waited for the perfect time to get started or listened to others on what I should have done.

Don't be like the mediocre majority. Instead, make a plan, get those around you involved in it or at least sign off on it, and then get to work.

While I can't promise you instant riches or overnight success, I can promise you that you won't be like the rest of them wondering "what if" on their death bed.

Life is too short a fragile to wait another second to get started.

Now is the time for you to make your dreams a reality.

And I'd love to hear about your success or help you with your struggles. You can reach me personally anytime via email - contacttimcastleman@gmail.com

Until next time.

Tim Castleman

Don't Forget My Free Gift To You

If you would like a free workbook, along with a 30 minute video and audio of me personally walking you through the 2kH Formula please visit: http://www.2khFormula.com/freegift

Once there, please provide a quality email address and I'll send you the workbook and walk-through video as my way of saying thanks and purchasing this book.

See you over at http://www.2khFormula.com/freegift

Tim

So ... What Did You Think?

I'd love to get your feedback on the 2kH Formula in the form of a review. Your positive reviews keep me inspired and motivated to write more and share my journey with you.

You can do a review by simply flipping to the end of this book or clicking on this link: http://www.timreallylikes.com/2kHreview

Once you leave your review, please take a screen shot of it and email me at contacttimcastleman@gmail.com. I have a gift for you that I only share with those who leave reviews.

http://timreallylikes.com/creativitychecklist

www.ingramcontent.com/pod-product-compliance
Lightning Source LLC
Chambersburg PA
CBHW021416170526
45164CB00002B/674